SCHIRMER'S LIBRARY OF MUSICAL CLASSICS

Vol. 1982

FRANZ JOSEPH HAYDN

Piano Sonatas

IN TWO BOOKS

▶ Book 1 — Library Vol. 1982

Book 2 — Library Vol. 1983

ISBN 0-7935-2657-4

G. SCHIRMER, Inc.

DISTRIBUTED BY

7777 W. BLUEMOUND RD. P.O. BOX 13819 MILWAUKEE, WI 53213

Copyright © 1993 by G. Schirmer, Inc. (ASCAP) New York, NY
International Copyright Secured. All Rights Reserved.
Warning: Unauthorized reproduction of this publication is
prohibited by Federal law and subject to criminal prosecution.

CONTENTS
Volume I

CONTENTS
Volume II

This newly prepared publication of the Complete Piano Sonatas of Franz Joseph Haydn (1732-1809) is intended for both performance and study. The term "complete" is, unfortunately, a bit of a misnomer. The scholarly debates concerning authenticity, compositional content and integrity, editorial markings, dates of creation and publication, and dedications—just to mention a few!—have been raging for nearly two hundred years. While these debates will certainly influence the choices an editor makes in any edition of Haydn's music, the purpose and scope of this edition does not propose to enter deeply into these debates. Our principle efforts have been in the subtle elimination of notational matters that may not be clear for twentieth-century performers and scholars. This edition is based on the original text edited by Karl Päsler (Gesamtausgabe of Haydn's works), and the order of the Sonatas follows the standard Hoboken numbering. On the title page of each Sonata is the Hoboken number ("Hob:"), the Feder/Grove reference ("G:"), and the Landon/Wiener Urtext number ("WU:").

SONATA
(Partita/Divertimento)

SONATA

Hob:2
G:Doubtful
WU:11

before 1765

12

Menuetto

a) ~

SONATA
(Divertimento)

Hob:3
G:3
WU:14

Allegro

before 1765

SONATA
(Divertimento)

SONATA

Hob:5
G:Doubtful
WU:8

appeared 1763

SONATA

Hob:6
G:1
WU:13

Allegro

appeared 1766

Finale
Allegro

SONATA
(Divertimento)

Hob:8
G:Doubtful
WU:1

1766

SONATA
(Divertimento)

Hob:9
G:Doubtful
WU:3

1766

SONATA

SONATA

Hob:11
G:Doubtful
WU:5

appeared 1767

Da Capo (al 𝄐)

SONATA

SONATA

Hob:13
G:Doubtful
WU:15

appeared 1767

Finale
Presto

SONATA

Hob:14
G:2
WU:16

appeared 1767

82

SONATA

Hob:15
G:Doubtful
WU:None

before 1785

SONATA

Hob:16
G:Doubtful
WU:None

before 1768

Minuetto

Minuetto da capo

SONATA

Hob:17
G:Doubtful
WU:None

before 1750–55

110

SONATA

Hob:18
G:17
WU:20

Allegro moderato

before 1767

SONATA

Finale
Allegro assai

a) ∽

SONATA

To the sisters Caterina and Marianna von Auenbrugger

Hob:20
G:36
WU:33

Moderato [Allegro moderato]

1771

Andante con moto

SONATA

To Prince Nicolaus Esterhazy

Hob:22
G:20
WU:37

Allegro moderato

1773

166

SONATA

To Prince Nicolaus Esterhazy

Hob:23
G:21
WU:38

[Allegro moderato]

1773

a)

171

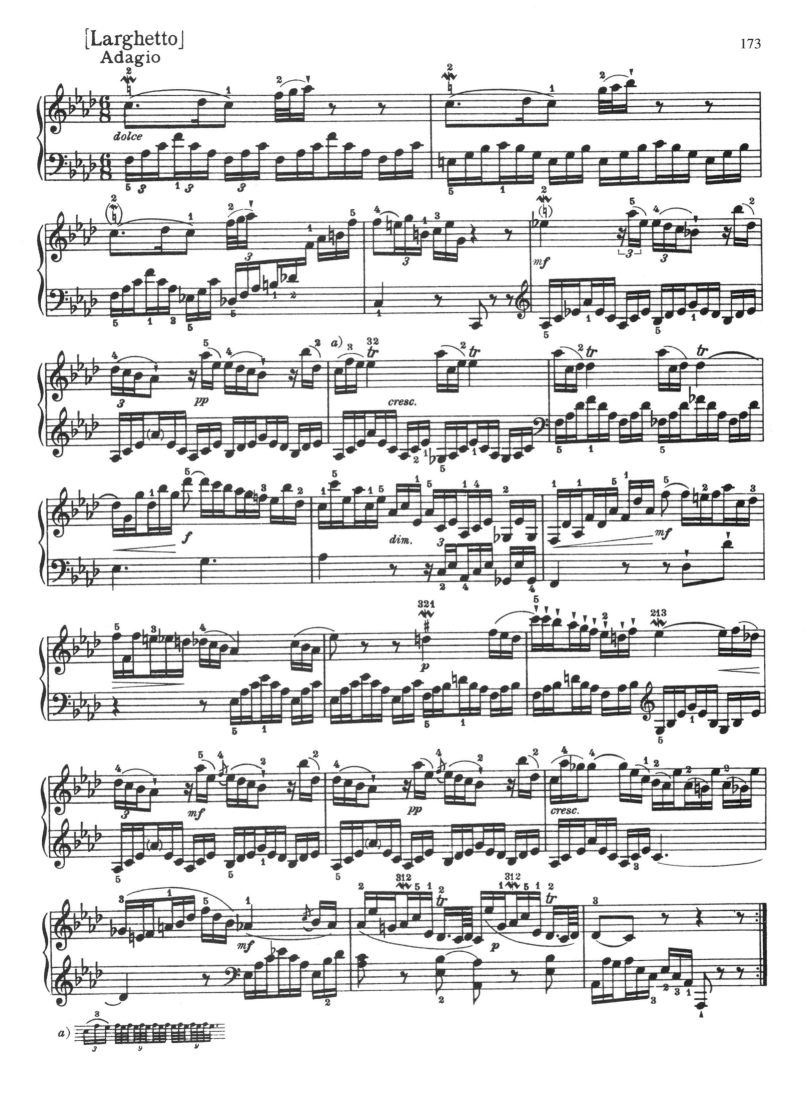

SONATA

To Prince Nicolaus Esterhazy

Hob:24
G:22
WU:39

1773

SONATA
To Prince Nicolaus Esterhazy

Hob:25
G:23
WU:40

Moderato

1773

a) $\;$ b) =

200

Finale
Presto

SONATA

Hob:27
G:25
WU:42

Franz Joseph Haydn
(1732-1809)
appeared 1776

Allegro con brio

Finale
Presto

SONATA

Hob:29
G:27
WU:44

appeared 1776

226

SONATA

Hob:30
G:28
WU:45

Allegro

appeared 1776